Let's Get Mapping!

Mapping Communities

Melanie Waldron

Raintree is an imprint of Capstone Global Library Limited, a company incorporated in England and Wales having its registered office at 7 Pilgrim Street, London, EC4V 6LB – Registered company number: 6695582

To contact Raintree please phone 0845 6044371, fax + 44 (0) 1865 312263, or email myorders@ raintreepublishers.co.uk. Customers from outside the UK please telephone +44 1865 312262.

Text © Capstone Global Library Limited 2013
First published in hardback in 2013
First published in paperback in 2014
The moral rights of the proprietor have been asserted.

Edited by Nancy Dickmann and Abby Colich
Designed by Victoria Allen
Original illustrations © 2013
Illustrated by HL Studios
Picture research by Ruth Blair
Originated by Capstone Global Library Limited
Printed and bound in China by CTPS

ISBN 978 1 406 24919 4 (hardback)
16 15 14 13 12
10 9 8 7 6 5 4 3 2 1

ISBN 978 1 406 24926 2 (paperback)
17 16 15 14 13
10 9 8 7 6 5 4 3 2 1

British Library Cataloguing in Publication Data
Waldron, Melanie.
Mapping communities. -- (Let's get mapping!)
526-dc23
A full catalogue record for this book is available from the British Library.

Acknowledgements

We would like to thank the following for permission to reproduce photographs: Alamy: pp. 4 (© Andrew Rubtsov), 13 (© Colin Underhill), 14 (© PURPLE MARBLES), 17 (© David R. Frazier Photolibrary, Inc.), 20 (© Corbis Cusp), 22 (© NetPhotos), 23 (© Robert Matton AB), 24 (© Ivy Close Images), 26 (© Wildscape); Corbis: p. 25 (© MAPS.com); 16 Designed and produced for Brighton & Hove bus company by FWT – www.fwt.co.uk; 15 © Lovell Johns Ltd 2012; Shutterstock: pp. 5 (© Songquan Deng), 6 (© RDaniel), 14 (© Mark Yuill), 19 (© Karin Hildebrand Lau), 27 (© Dmitry Kalinovsky), 28 (© photobank.ch).

Background images and design features reproduced with permission from Shutterstock.

Cover photograph of an illustrated, aerial street map reproduced with permission of Shutterstock (© Robert Adrian Hillman).

Every effort has been made to contact copyright holders of material reproduced in this book. Any omissions will be rectified in subsequent printings if notice is given to the publisher.

All the internet addresses (URLs) given in this book were valid at the time of going to press. However, due to the dynamic nature of the internet, some addresses may have changed, or sites may have changed or ceased to exist since publication. While the author and publisher regret any inconvenience this may cause readers, no responsibility for any such changes can be accepted by either the author or the publisher.

Contents

Some words appear in the text in bold, **like this**. You can find out what they mean by looking in the glossary.

What is a map?

You have probably used some maps already. You will know that they are usually flat and that they contain some information about the land. There are all sorts of different maps. People use some maps, such as road and rail maps, to help them plan journeys. Other maps can help us to find places or addresses. Some maps can contain information that helps us to learn about different countries.

People use maps for lots of different reasons. Maps can help us to find places and work out the best way to get to them.

This is a bird's eye view of the land – just what a bird might see!

A bird's eye view

Most maps show what the land looks like from above. This is called a **bird's eye view**. Some maps are all about the **natural features** of Earth – for example the hills, mountains, rivers, and lakes. Other maps are all about the world that humans have created – for example cities, towns, and buildings.

MAPPING WORDS

Different types of maps can be called charts or plans. People who make maps are called **cartographers**, and map making is called **cartography**.

A world of communities

This book is about mapping **communities**. A community is a group of people with something in common. For example, your class is a community. You can be part of many different communities: your school, your street, your sports club, or your town.

Communities can be very small. They can be made up of just a few people. They can also be huge! Even your country is a community.

These children are playing football. They are all part of this small community.

Maps for communities

Different communities need different things. Maps can help to make sure that communities have the things they need. For example, imagine a community was planning to build a new playground. They would have to make sure that it was near to houses or schools, so that children would not have to walk too far to get to it.

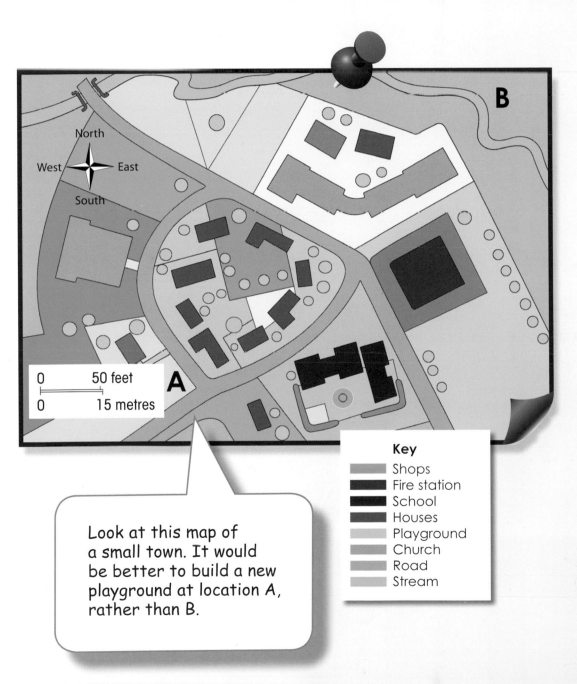

Look at this map of a small town. It would be better to build a new playground at location A, rather than B.

Key
- Shops
- Fire station
- School
- Houses
- Playground
- Church
- Road
- Stream

Maps for small communities

Very small communities might want to make a map of one room! The map might show where seating areas, doors, play areas, or quiet areas are. Maps like this are useful for planning how best to use the space. They are also useful when new furniture or equipment is being brought in.

A map of a youth-club room is useful for deciding where different activities should be held.

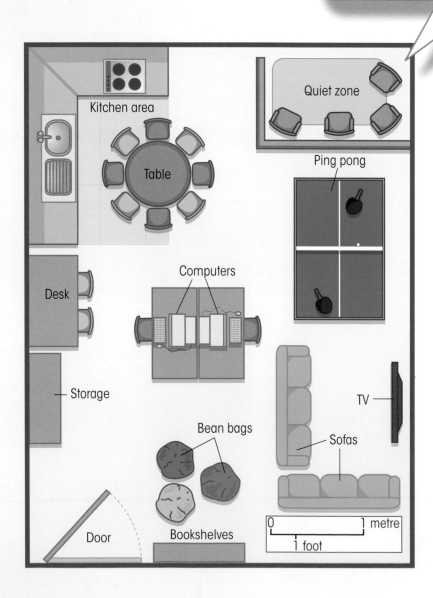

Kitchen area

Table

Quiet zone

Ping pong

Computers

Desk

Storage

TV

Bean bags

Sofas

Door

Bookshelves

0   1 metre

1 foot

Mapping buildings

Maps of buildings, such as hospitals, are also very useful for small communities. They can show all the rooms in the building, and what each room is used for. They can show really important information such as the location of emergency exits and other doors. They can help people to find toilets and kitchens.

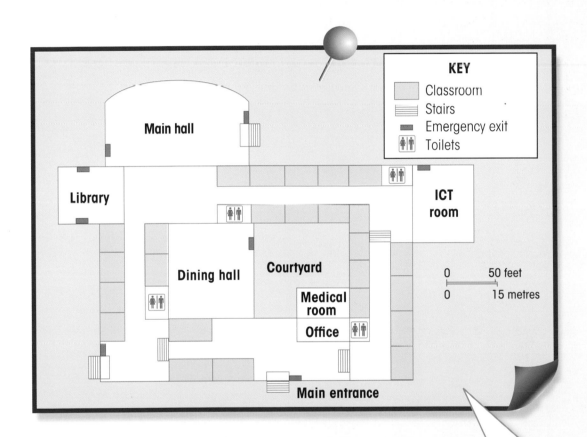

KEY
- Classroom
- Stairs
- Emergency exit
- Toilets

Main hall

Library

ICT room

Dining hall

Courtyard

Medical room

Office

Main entrance

0   50 feet
0   15 metres

This is a map of a school. A school map is very useful for new pupils. It can help them find their way around.

NOT TOO CLOSE!

Some playground equipment needs a lot of space. For example, you wouldn't want to put a slide right in front of a swing! People planning playgrounds use maps to make sure that all the equipment is placed a safe distance apart.

A sense of scale

You will notice that there is a lot more detail on the youth-club room map than on the school map. This is because the youth-club room map is at a larger **scale** than the school map. Larger scale means a smaller area, but more detail. A very **large-scale map**, such as a map of your teacher's desk, could show even more detail! For example, it could show where the pens and pencils are kept.

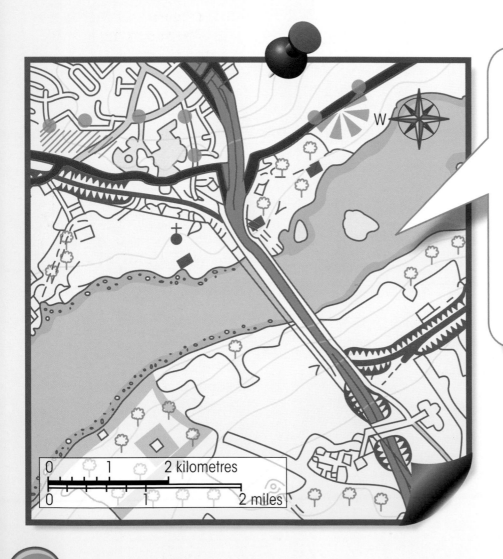

This is a large-scale map. It covers only a small area of the map opposite, but it shows lots more detail about the land. There are many more roads and buildings shown on this map.

0   1   2 kilometres

0   1   2 miles

All maps shrink down everything in the real world. We call this scaling down. **Small-scale maps** shrink things down a lot. They can show large areas of land, such as a whole country. But they can't show much detail. A road map for a country would be an example of a small-scale map.

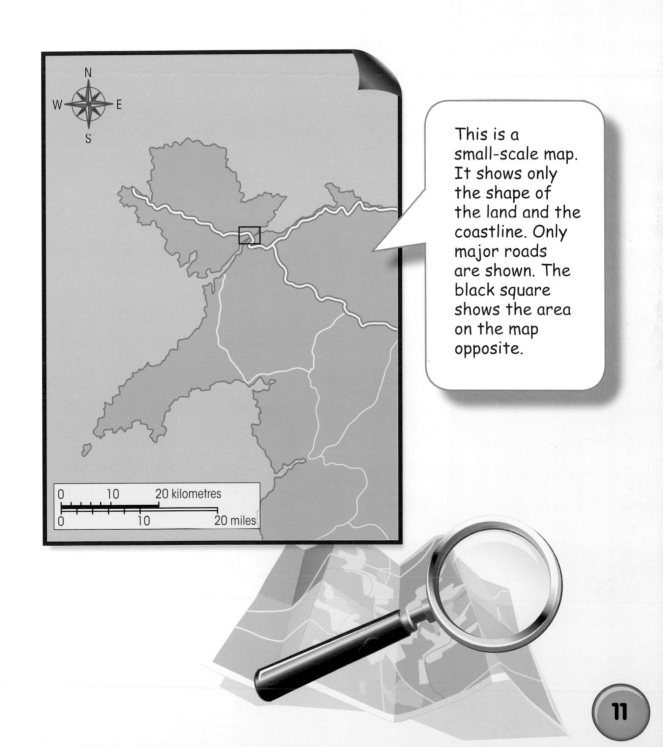

This is a small-scale map. It shows only the shape of the land and the coastline. Only major roads are shown. The black square shows the area on the map opposite.

Maps for larger communities

A map of your neighbourhood would show less detail than a map of your school, but it would cover a larger area of land. It might show all the streets in your area. It might also show the houses, shops, parks, and other buildings.

A map of a town could show useful information, such as the location of libraries, hospitals, schools, and dentists. It could also show shopping areas, housing areas, train stations, and bus stops.

This is a map of Windsor town centre. It shows the main roads and some important buildings.

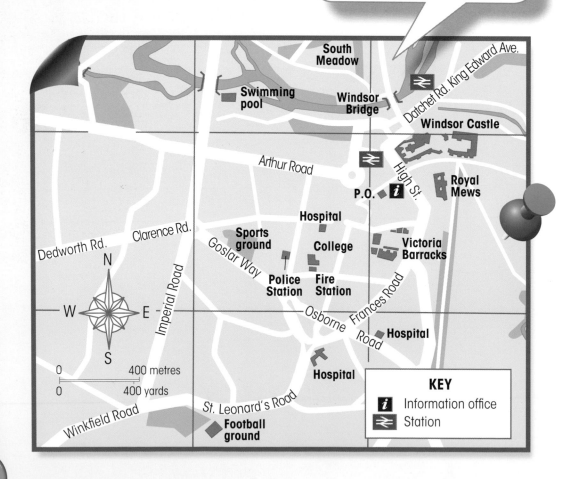

Pictorial maps

Some towns have **pictorial maps** made of them. These maps have tiny drawings of the buildings in the town. They are attractive to look at and they can help people find their way around. They are often used in areas where lots of tourists visit.

FUN MAPS

Some theme parks and zoos also use pictorial maps to help people find things. They have drawings of the animals and the rides. These maps are fun to use and take home afterwards!

Which way now?

When you are using a map of your community, it is important to make sure you can read it! One of the first things to do is to check that the map is the right way round. This means that North on the map must be the same as North in real life.

Most maps have a **compass rose** printed on them so you can tell which way is North. The compass rose will show where North, South, East, and West are on the map. Some maps simply have an arrow to show which way is North.

Most compass roses show North, South, East, and West.

You can use a **compass** to find where North is in real life.

Street plans

Maps that show all the streets in an area are called **street plans**. They are very useful for walking or driving around. They give all the names of the streets to help you understand where you are and how to get to where you want to go.

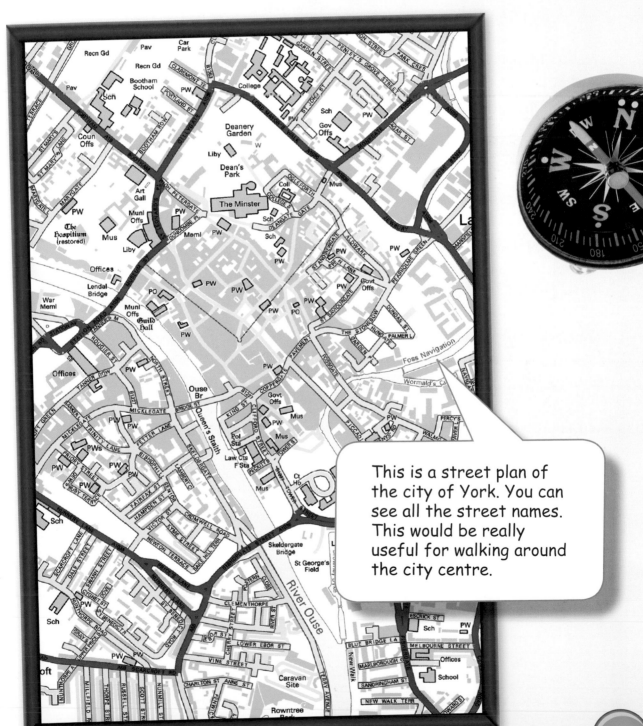

This is a street plan of the city of York. You can see all the street names. This would be really useful for walking around the city centre.

Getting around

If you want to use public transport to get around your community then you would need to use transport maps. There are different kinds of transport maps. Your area might have maps of bus, tram, or train routes. For each type of map, it is also useful to see where the stations and stops are, so that you can plan where to get on and off.

> This map shows the bus routes around Brighton. There is another map for the city centre, because all the detail would be hard to show on this map.

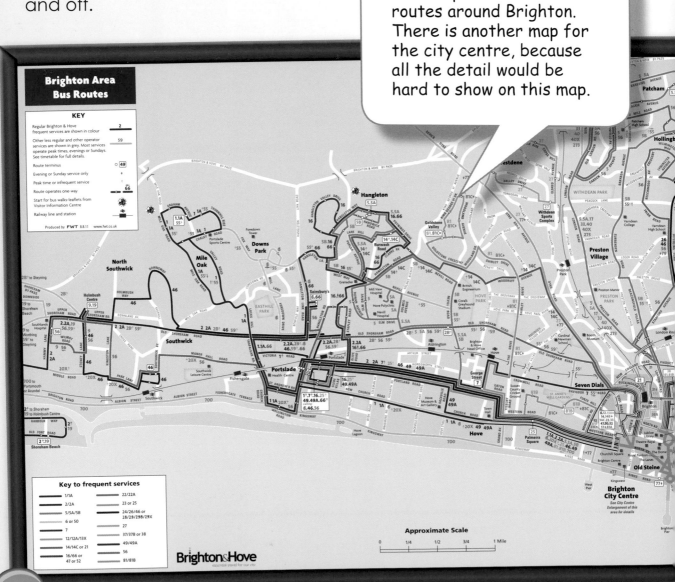

Simple maps

Some transport maps, such as the London Underground map, don't show the road or train routes like they are in real life. The routes are straightened and the distances between the stops are equally spaced. This is because you don't really need to know about all the bends and distances in the route – you just need to know how to get from one bus or train station to another! These maps make it easier to plan a journey because they are very simple.

This is a map of the underground train system in Washington, DC, USA. The routes have been straightened and the stations are evenly spaced apart.

How far is it?

When you use a map of your community, it is useful to be able to work out the distances between places. Most maps have a **scale bar** printed on them to help you do this. A scale bar is a bar, or a line, with numbers printed along it.

You can measure the distance on the map, perhaps with a ruler. You can then hold the ruler against the scale bar to see how far this distance is in real life.

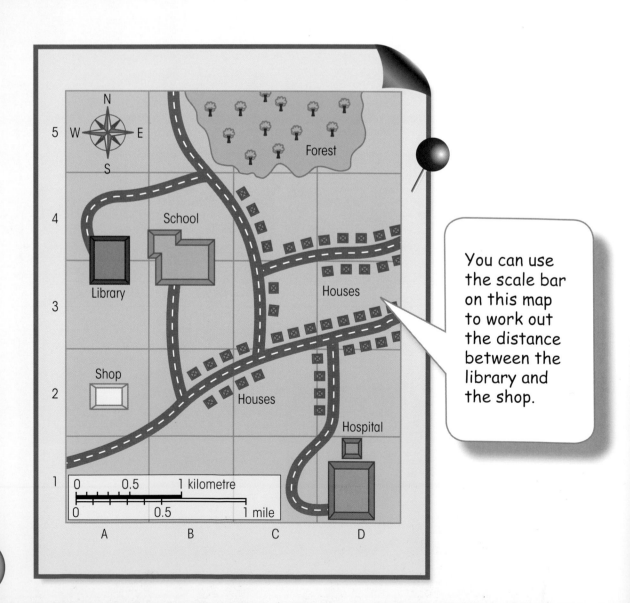

You can use the scale bar on this map to work out the distance between the library and the shop.

Gridlines

You will see that there is a grid printed on the map. You can use **gridlines** to find places on a map. Every square made by the grid has a **grid reference**. Use the letters across the bottom for the first part of the grid reference. Use the numbers up the side for the second part. For example, the hospital has a grid reference of D1.

REAL LIFE GRIDS

Some towns and cities, especially in the United States, are built on a grid system. This means that their streets look like a grid on a map.

Using maps

You can use maps of your community in different ways. You can use them to find where important places are, or to work out the best way to get to places. You can use them to learn about places that are new to you.

Before you use a map of your community, you should look at its title. This will tell you what the map is trying to show you. For example, if a map only shows the schools in the area, it would not be much use for finding anything else!

Maps can help you explore your community.

Map symbols

Maps that show lots of different things often use **symbols**. These are little drawings or shapes that represent different things on the map. For example, a black line might represent a railway and a blue line might represent a river. A tree could represent a forest and a slide could represent a playground.

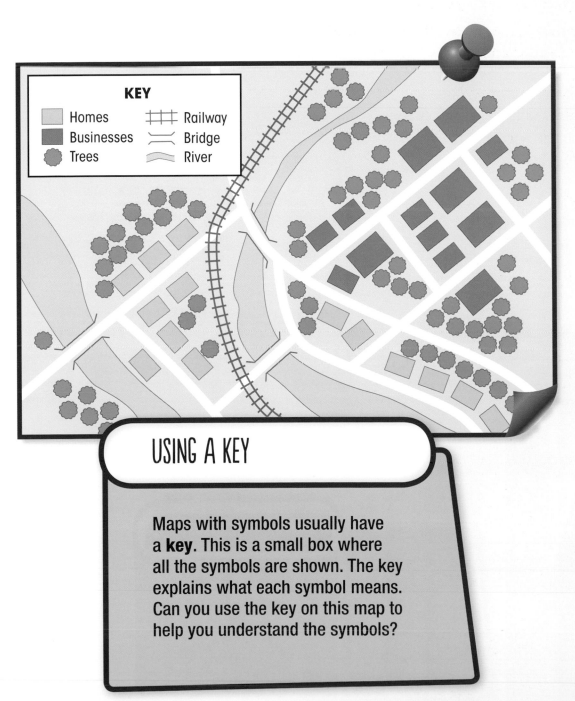

KEY

▢	Homes	╫╫	Railway
▢	Businesses	⌇	Bridge
✿	Trees	∿	River

USING A KEY

Maps with symbols usually have a **key**. This is a small box where all the symbols are shown. The key explains what each symbol means. Can you use the key on this map to help you understand the symbols?

Online maps

You can find maps of all types on the internet. These **online** maps are very useful because many of them have search tools. You can search for postcodes, addresses, and building names. Online maps can help you find exactly what you are looking for. For example, if you put "swimming pools" in the search box, the computer can show you all the swimming pools in your area.

STREET VIEW

Google is a huge internet company. You can explore its map section, Google Maps. When you find your area, you can drag the little yellow person onto the map. This will change the map to a "street view" of the area. You can then look at all the streets and buildings in your area. You can move along the street and turn around to see the view from all directions.

Many mapping websites have several features to help you figure out where you're going.

Moving maps

Satellites above Earth can send signals to devices such as **satnav** systems in cars and mobile phones. These pick up the signals and can work out exactly where you are. They show a map of the area where you are with your position marked on it. The maps change as you move about.

Satnav systems can make it really easy to find places and stop you from getting lost!

Maps in history

Maps are extremely useful for seeing how places have changed over time. You can look at old maps of your community to see how towns and cities have grown larger. These maps can also help you find the oldest parts of your community. Very modern maps can show you the newest parts of your community.

This map of Rome is at least 1,700 years old.

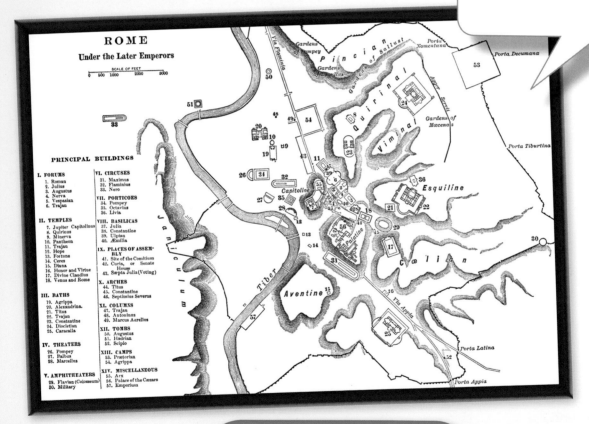

OLDEST TOWN MAP

There is an ancient wall painting in Turkey, showing the streets and houses of a settlement. Scientists think it is about 8,000 years old, making it the oldest town map in the world.

This map shows the same area of Rome today.

The shapes of towns

Historical maps can help to explain the location of some towns and cities. Many historical **settlements** were built near rivers, so people could use boats to travel and transport things. Some towns grew up where two rivers meet, or where it was easy to build a bridge to cross a river. Other towns grew up along ancient roads.

Maps can also explain more modern settlements. Some very long, thin towns are that shape because the buildings have grown along the sides of roads.

Making maps today

For hundreds of years, maps were mostly made using sketches of the land. Sometimes, people would climb to the highest point in the area, such as a church tower, to get the best view of the land.

Today, most maps are made using **aerial photographs** and **satellite images**. Aerial photographs are taken by cameras attached to aeroplanes. These aeroplanes fly backwards and forwards over the land. Satellites capture images of Earth from space. Satellite images can cover huge areas.

Small aeroplanes such as this one have powerful cameras mounted onto them. They fly back and forth taking photographs of the areas of land they pass over.

More detail

Maps of communities may need a bit more detail than an aerial photograph or satellite image can provide. Specially trained people called **surveyors** make the most accurate maps of towns and cities. Surveyors use special instruments to measure exact distances and locations.

This surveyor is using a tool called a **theodolite**. It is used to measure the angles between things.

Get mapping!

Why not make a map of your school and playground? Imagine that the map is for a new pupil. You need to decide what things would be important for them to know about. For example, you could include the emergency exits, toilets, school canteen, and school office. Once you have decided what to include, you need to work out how you will show the information on your map. Will you simply label everything, or will you use symbols and a key? Remember to give your map a title.

What's at the end of this corridor? A map of the building would tell you.

The perfect town

Now design the perfect place to live. Draw a map of your ideal town, including all the things you would like to have there. Where would you like all these things to be? Remember that you should include important places like a school and a library. You could add a title, scale bar, north arrow, and a key to complete your map.

What would you include in your ideal town?

BE A SURVEYOR!

If you want to work as a surveyor, you usually need to go to university. You can choose from lots of different courses that include surveying. You would then need to work as a trainee for two or three years before becoming fully qualified.

Glossary

aerial photograph photograph taken from high above Earth's surface, usually from an aeroplane

bird's eye view the way something looks from high up – as it might be seen by a bird flying overhead

cartographer person who makes maps

cartography making maps

community group of people living close to each other, or having shared interests

compass instrument with a needle that always points North

compass rose drawing with four points, showing where North, South, East, and West are on a map

gridlines lines going both across and up and down a map, forming a grid

grid reference figure made up of numbers and letters, or just numbers, that allows you to pinpoint a place on a map

key list of symbols and an explanation of what each one represents

large-scale map map that shows a small area in a lot of detail

natural feature something on Earth's surface that has been created by nature, for example a mountain

online something that is found on the internet

pictorial map map with tiny drawings of the features it wants to show, often used in popular tourist places

satellite spacecraft that travels around Earth and gathers or sends back information

satellite image picture, like a photograph, that a satellite can take of Earth from space

satnav short for "satellite navigation", which means using signals from satellites to help us find our location

scale the amount a map is shrunk down from real life

scale bar bar or line on a map which shows how far a distance on the map represents in real life

settlement collection of houses where people live

small-scale map map that shows a large area but without much detail

street plan large-scale map of an area that names all the streets

surveyor person who takes measurements of streets and buildings

symbol small picture on a map that represents a familiar feature of a town or landscape. For example, a red cross might represent a hospital.

theodolite tool used by surveyors to measure angles up and down, and left to right

Find out more

There is a whole world of maps and mapping waiting to be discovered! Begin by looking at these books and websites.

Books

Cities, Towns, and Villages (Mapping Britain's Landscape), Barbara Taylor (Franklin Watts, 2012)

Introducing Maps (Maps and Mapping Skills), Meg and Jack Gillett (Wayland, 2010)

Mapping Towns and Cities (Mapping Our World), Robert Walker (Marshall Cavendish, 2010)

Where We Live (Using Maps), Susan Hoe (TickTock Books, 2009)

Websites

www.bing.com/maps
On this site, you can find maps of places all over the world. You can click a button called "Bird's eye" to see what the land actually looks like.

maps.google.co.uk
On Google's mapping website, Google Maps, you can find maps of any area in the world. You can zoom in and out, and use the little yellow person to view land from the ground.

mapzone.ordnancesurvey.co.uk/mapzone/index.html
This is an interactive site all about maps and mapping, with homework help, maps, photos, and games. The teaching resources section includes lots of useful sheets about map skills.

www.streetmap.co.uk
This mapping website will find any place in the UK. Just enter a postcode, street name, or town name in the search box and it will go to that area. You can then zoom in or out to get the detail you need.

Index